CONTE

MISSION STATEMENT FOR THE FREEDOM PROGRAMME

Any woman should be able to phone the contact numbers on my website and be told where and when the next session is taking place and whether crèche facilities are available. I do not endorse intrusive questions, referrals or risk assessments.

Women must be actively welcomed to the programme.

We never give advice or tell any woman that she should leave. If it were so easy we would have all left.

Judgemental statements such as 'I would never let anyone do that to me' or 'this has never happened to me' are not acceptable.

Facilitators refer to all women as 'us' and never use the dreaded words 'These Women'.

These programmes are only for the women who attend them. I do not endorse the presence of observers.

Ideally, every woman who attends should be given a copy of the book 'Living with the Dominator' and the supplement 'The Freedom Programme Home Study Course' as soon as she arrives. This will enhance her learning. Clearly **she** will know if it is safe to take these publications home or to leave them in a folder with the facilitator.

This programme lasts for 12 x 90 minute sessions. It is a rolling programme, so women who attend can miss a session and do it later when they are ready. Some women can take years to complete it. Session 4 is about the 'Effects of Domestic Abuse on Children'. It is repeated in session 8. Facilitators who only want to run this once can shorten the programme to 11 weeks.

 freedomprogramme@btinternet.com
www.freedomprogramme.co.uk

Session 1. The Dominator (Chapter 2, Pages 9 - 16)

1.1. Introductions and 'ice breaker'

Welcome everyone and give out the books. Clearly, everyone will know if it is safe to take them home or not. Emphasise that no one is to say 'I have never experienced any abuse'. This statement is guaranteed to make all those of us who have experienced it feel instantly inferior!

I count everyone in to their groups using names. For example, I may choose Daffodils, Tulips, Roses and Daisies. Give everyone a name then direct all the Daffodils to one group of chairs, Tulips to another and so on.

In small groups, please ask the members to introduce themselves to their companions in our 'Freedom Programme' way. Ask them to: 'Think of your first name then think of a really wonderful description of yourself which begins with the same initial as your name. Then add any place in the universe which is where you come from'. For example: 'I am Perfect Pat and I come from Paradise'. It is often hard to think of these positive names so the group may need some help. For example: if I say 'I am Dismal Dora from Dorking' the group should lovingly rename me 'Delightful Dora'. This serves the dual purpose of making us laugh and helping us to begin to feel better about ourselves.

 freedomprogramme@btinternet.com
www.freedomprogramme.co.uk

1.2. Group Rules

In the first week of the programme the facilitator leads this exercise by asking the group which rules they want for their group to make this a safe and comfortable experience. In the following weeks, the group members take charge of this and introduce new women to the process.

One person - One voice

The Freedom Programme is a group work programme. We work together in small groups. This enables us to learn from each other by sharing our knowledge and experience. To function as a group we need to speak one at a time and listen to each other.

Confidentiality

Everything said in this room stays in here. We do not greet each other if we unexpectedly meet outside. However, we do exchange mobile numbers and make friends. The group members remind each other every week that, if someone reveals that a child is being hurt, the facilitator **will** alert child protection agencies. Be aware that this sort of disclosure is **NEVER** accidental.

Caution

We may begin to realise how very abusive our current partner actually is. It is wise not to challenge him. Complete the course. Knowledge is power. If you are thinking of leaving, try to plan carefully. The programme facilitators can provide practical assistance.

No advice

No one should ever tell anyone to leave the relationship or make judgemental remarks such as: 'I would never put up with that'.

Agree to differ

During the programme we all discuss a series of questions but there are no absolute answers. The aim of the programme is to help us to think about and question our society and ourselves. The facilitators are not here to give their personal opinions.

Feelings
This experience can be painful. We all need to realise this and give each other lots of love and kindness.

Timing
About half the session deals with answering the questions and the rest is devoted to feedback and discussion.

Fun
Women who have done the programme have said that the sessions are fun.

Mobile phones
We do not have to switch them off. This can enrage our Dominator.

1.3. History

The facilitator reads the history from book 'Living with the Dominator'. This is found on pages 5 - 7.

1.4. Statistics Quiz

As a woman who comes to the Programme for the first time, I will probably believe that I am the only woman who is experiencing this. Consequentially, I will probably believe that I am causing it to happen. I need to know the statistics so I will realise that I am not alone. Statistics can be boring so we have put them in the form of a quiz.

Read out the questions to all the groups. Then ask them to discuss each one and to come to a consensus. Give each group a chance to answer.

Statistic quiz. Week 1 only

The facilitator asks the groups to discuss these statistics in the form of a quiz.

The Quiz

1. Domestic violence accounts for:

2% ☐ 10% ☐ 25% ☐

of all reported violent crime.

2. In Britain, a woman is killed by a violent partner or former partner every:

3 days ☐ week ☐ 2 weeks ☐

3. It is estimated that:

3% ☐ 13% ☐ 33% ☐

of all women experience domestic violence in their lifetime.

4. How many times, on average, is a woman assaulted before she seeks help?

5 ☐ 15 ☐ 35 ☐

5. On average, how many men a year are killed by their female partners or former partners?

22 ☐ 52 ☐ 112 ☐

6. On average, how many women a year are killed by their male partners or former partners?

12 ☐ 52 ☐ 112 ☐

7. How many women's refuges are there in England?

275 ☐ 1000 ☐ 5000 ☐

8. Is a woman:

less likely ☐ just as likely ☐ more likely ☐

to be assaulted when she is pregnant?

9. Domestic violence happens because of:

drink ☐ drugs ☐ stress ☐ mental illness ☐

unemployment ☐ none of these ☐

10. In Britain, police receive a complaint about domestic violence every:

60 seconds ☐ 6 minutes ☐ 6 hours ☐

11. In Britain, a woman is assaulted in her home every:

6 seconds ☐ 60 seconds ☐ 6 minutes ☐

THE ANSWERS

1. 25% of all reported crime (Amnesty UK, 2006)

2. Every 3 days (Home Office, 2007)

3. 33% (Home Office 2007). My experience with the Freedom Programme leads me to believe it is higher. Many of us do not realise we are being abused.

4. 35 (Amnesty UK, 2006)

5. 22 (Home Office, 2007)

6. 112 (Home Office, 2007)

7. 275 (Women's Aid, 2004) and, approximately, 1500 animal refuges

8. 3 times more likely to be injured when pregnant (Refuge, 2007)

9. None of these

10. 60 seconds (Day to count, *Elizabeth E. Stanko,* 2000)

11. 6 seconds (Day to count, *Elizabeth E. Stanko,* 2000)

1.5 The Dominator and Mr Right

You will see from the statistics that most abusers are men and that they use abusive behaviour to keep us women under control. Now, tell the group members to open their books at the picture of the Dominator on page 11. Talk the groups through each type of abuse. You can then add more examples of each type of abuse for each group. If there is time, each group can invite one member to write down these examples. Then, ask the groups to share the new examples with the other groups.

When you have done this turn to page 14 and read out the last paragraph, which introduces Mr Right on page 15. Read all the examples of non-abusive behaviour.

Remind participants that the purpose of the Mr. Right handout is to reinforce the message that the behaviour of the Dominator is abusive and not 'normal'.

We will return to study him in greater detail later in the course.

In the next part of the session, facilitators assist the group members to begin to understand why abusive men want to control women. To achieve this, facilitators explain the difference between thoughts and beliefs. The facilitators explain to the group members that everyone behaves the way they do because of what they believe, not because of what they think. The group is invited to discuss the difference between a thought and a belief. Beliefs are the engines that drive our behaviour. When we start to get to know our beliefs we start to understand ourselves.

We often do not see our beliefs as beliefs. We see them as facts.

1.6 Beliefs awareness exercise

A facilitator asks all members to stand and form a circle. A facilitator will invite group members to step into the centre of the circle if they hold the sentiments expressed in this exercise. Remember to ask them to step back out again after each question.

Do I believe it is important to keep the air we breathe clean?
Do I drive a car?
If the answer to both questions is yes, what do I really believe about my needs and the needs of the planet?

Do I disapprove of bullying?
Have I ever shouted at my children, partner or the dog?
If the answer to both questions is yes, what do I really believe about bullying?

If group members respond to both (and most will) they will also recognise that they believe that bullying works and it is acceptable if you have a good excuse.

I give the example of shouting at the dog who has messed on the carpet.

Beliefs are: I own the dog. I am superior. The dog is inferior. Bullying works.

Bullying is fine if you can justify it. Remind everyone that the Bully also holds these beliefs.

Do I believe in keeping my body healthy?
Do I smoke, drink or eat too much?
If the answer to both questions is yes, what do I really believe? Most of the group will respond to this and then I usually use my former addiction to cigarettes to illustrate these beliefs. Together, we will agree that when I smoked I believed that although cigarettes did kill other people, I did not believe they would kill me. This example of holding two conflicting or irrational beliefs can be compared to the dissonant beliefs of abusive men. This is 'cognitive dissonance.'

Do I believe women have a right to say no to sex?
Have I ever made a feeble excuse?
The facilitator should point out that, if this last example is used, we may well believe that we do not, in fact, have the right to say no to sex. We will return to this theme later in the programme.

The beliefs of the Dominator

At this point, group members are invited to consider which beliefs abusive men hold. We will identify that the Dominator believes that it is OK to use violence if you have a good excuse and that it is acceptable to use such violence to control women. We will recognise that he believes women are inferior beings who need to be controlled.

I then ask the group where such beliefs come from. They will suggest childhood and society and we will begin to discuss how they are reinforced by the society in which we live. I emphasise that the Dominator is not a deviant but, is in fact, enacting the beliefs of the society in which *he* lives.

 freedomprogramme@btinternet.com
www.freedomprogramme.co.uk

I then ask: ' who else in our society is exposed to the same influences as the abuser?' The answer is of course that we women are conditioned in the same way. I then lay the ground for the rest of the programme by explaining that most of the sessions will examine the tactics used by each aspect of the Dominator, the beliefs which motivate the tactics, the origins and which beliefs women share.

I add that we will also end all sessions on a positive note, usually discussing the attributes of a non- abusive man.

1.7 Why Do Women Not Go Back to Abusive Men?

Staying in the large group, the facilitator invites women to offer suggestions as to how a woman's life is improved when the Dominator is no longer in the home. What can we do now that we could not do before? This is more powerful when we answer in the first person. e.g. 'I can cuddle my children'.

Session 2. The Bully (Chapter 3, Pages 17 - 25)

From now on, this is the format for each session.
Put everyone into small groups. Introduce groups with the Freedom names.

2.1

Welcome everyone back. Welcome new members and introduce them to the Dominator and Mr Right. Give them their books. Ask an experienced group member to look after each new arrival. Ask the group to remind each other of the rules.

All the rest of the sessions begin with a quiz about the Dominator. Read a tactic and ask the groups to call out which aspect of the dominator uses each tactic. Remind everyone that the aim of the quiz is not so much to get all the answers right, but more to help us to identify and name abusive behaviour when we see it.

The Quiz

Tactic

1. Sulks
2. Tells me my tits are too small
3. Goes out of the room when my friends visit
4. Says 'It was only a push!'
5. Tells the kids I am stupid
6. Expects his dinner to be ready whenever he walks through the door
7. Invites my friend to have a threesome
8. Threatens to kill himself if I leave

Answers

1 The Bully
2. The Headworker
3. The Jailer
4. The Liar
5. The Badfather
6. The King of the Castle
7. The Sexual Controller
8. The Persuader

2.2 Question Sheets

2.2 Question Sheets for the Bully

These sheets are available to copy from this manual or to read from 'The Home Study Course'. If you use the 'Home Study Course' women will become accustomed to it and be more likely to use it to enhance their learning.
Invite the groups to allow one of their members to volunteer to make notes. Emphasise that we want volunteers not conscripts. Tell them that we also need one person in each group to read out questions from 'The Home Study Course' or from a hand out. Everyone else now must close their books.
Tell the groups to answer one section at a time and not to move on until the facilitator instructs them. Walk round and listen to make sure they all read out each question.

Tell the group members to answer all the questions in role. In most of the of the question sheets answer the first three questions in the role of the abuser.

e.g. A sample answer for the tactics of the Bully is'I shout'.
e.g. A sample answer for the beliefs of the Bully could be 'Women need to be kept in order'.
e.g. A sample answer for 'Where does the Bully get his beliefs could be 'Most religions do not allow women to be priests' which gives a strong message that we are not good enough.

When answering the next questions ask the groups to answer in role as a woman. Ask them to answer as 'every woman' and consider our beliefs before even meeting a bully.

This provides a safe space for anyone who wishes to talk about their own situation. No one should ask anyone else: 'Are you in role?'

e.g. A sample answer to the question
Which beliefs do I as a woman share?' could be 'Strong (dominating) men can be attractive.'

'How are women affected by being bullied'? could be
'I am walking on eggshells and can never relax'

Answer the last question in the role of the non abusive counterpart to the abusive man.
e.g. A sample answer to the question
'How does the friend behave?' could be
'I have a sense of humour and do not have to have the last word'.

Competing the quiz and answering the question sheets should take 30 minutes. The feedback should take 60 minutes.

Role play in the feedback.
Before taking the feedback invite the groups to give a name to the man they are role playing. This can produce much amusement and some very ingenious names.

 freedomprogramme@btinternet.com
www.freedomprogramme.co.uk

Question Sheet for session 2. The Bully.

The tactics of the Bully
Answer in role as the Bully.
Make a list of as many as you can think of.
We are not asking for examples of violence. Concentrate on intimidation.
How does the Bully use his body language to intimidate me?
How does he use every bit of his body?
Think of his fingers, toes and eyes.
Don't ask what he says, but how he says it?

What does the Bully believe?
Answer in role as the Bully.
What does he believe about violence, "real" men and the status of women compared to men? Does he believe I need controlling/protecting? What does he believe about men who do not bully?

Where do his beliefs come from and how are they reinforced?
Answer in role as the Bully.
What about culture, sports and institutions such as the armed forces?
Only discuss your OWN culture.
Consider religion, music and all forms of media including film.
Give examples.

Which of these beliefs do we women share?
Answer as every woman.
Do I believe I need looking after?
What sort of men do I fancy?

How are we affected by being bullied in this way?
Answer in the role of a woman.
How do I feel all the time?
How may I behave?

How does the Friend behave and what does he believe?
Answer in the role of the friend who is a non abusive man.
Look at his body language.
What are his eyes like? What is his voice like?
What does he believe about women?
Does he like women?
What does he believe about the use of violence?

2.3 Notes for the feedback

The beliefs of the Bully

One belief that is usually identified is that the Bully believes he is superior to women. As soon as this is identified, it has been found helpful to create him as an imaginary Dominator. He can be christened Roger, for example. The facilitator places Roger in an empty chair and invites participants to ask him questions and provide the answers for him.

The dialogue will begin by asking him why he is superior to women in general and his partner in particular. It will end when it becomes clear that this belief is founded on physical strength and the facilitators ensure that the final part of the dialogue makes clear that greater physical strength is not an indicator of greater ability.

Example of dialogue with Roger

"Tell me Roger why do you feel you are superior to women?"
"Because I earn the money in this family"
"But Roger, your partner actually earns more than you"
"Possibly, but I am more intelligent and do a more important job."
"So what about your partner's degree in Rocket Science as opposed to your NVQ level 1 in Painting and Decorating".
"But all she does is sit around all day writing and talking. I do real work."
"What do you mean by real work Roger? Surely she has more effect on more people than you?"
"I mean man's work, physical work".
"So what is it about this that makes you superior Roger?"
"I am stronger than her, I can lift more than her, and I can do more than her".
"So you believe that all physically strong creatures are superior to all less strong creatures?"
"Of course"
"So, Roger, why isn't there an elephant in the White House and a gorilla running Microsoft?"

Explain that Roger is conflating two distinct and different concepts. Physical strength and superiority are not the same.

Beliefs we women share

Read the Fairy Story from page 23.

Finish the session by reminding the group that the contents of this session are covered in pages 17 - 25 of 'Living with the Dominator'.

Session 3. The Badfather (Chapter 4, Pages 27 - 34)

3.1 The Quiz

Tactics

1. Smashes things
2. Tells other people my secrets
3. Tells me my friend made a pass at him
4. Says I started it
5. Uses the courts to get access to the children
6. Nags until I agree to sex
7. Takes all the money
8. Says he has nowhere else to go

Answers

1. The Bully
2. The Headworker
3. The Jailer
4. The Liar
5. The Badfather
6. The Sexual Controller
7. The King of the Castle
8. The Persuader

3.2. Question Sheet for Session 3. The Badfather

Tactics of the Badfather

Answer in the role of the Badfather.

How does the Badfather ensure that I cannot control the children?

How does he use the children to isolate me?

How does he use the children to persuade me to have him back after violence?

How does he use the children to intimidate me? He can do this when we are still together or when I have separated from him.

How will he use other agencies to use the children to abuse me?

His beliefs

Answer in the role of the Badfather.

What does he believe about childcare and real men?

Does he believe that women can cope with children without a man, any man, in the house?

Who does he think has rights? Women, children, or him?

Does he believe violence affects children? Does he care?

Origins and reinforcements

Answer in the role of the Badfather.

Where does he get his beliefs from?

Consider political propaganda.

Consider the messages he gets from the media about the need for a father figure

What do the family courts tell him?

What message does he get from pressure groups?

What messages has he had from other agencies?

 freedomprogramme@btinternet.com
www.freedomprogramme.co.uk

Which beliefs do we share?
Answer in the role of every woman.
Do I believe the children are not affected by his violence?
Do I believe I can cope with the children without a man or am I letting them down?

How are we affected?
Answer in the role of the mother.
How am I affected when he uses access and the courts to harass me?
How am I affected when he uses the children to isolate me?
How am I affected when he turns the children against me?

The Goodfather

Answer in the role of the Goodfather
How does the Goodfather behave towards me in front of the children?
How does he behave towards the children?
What does he believe about childcare?

Take the feedback then finish the session by reminding the group that the contents of this session are covered in pages 27 - 34 of 'Living with the Dominator'.

Session 4. The Effects of Domestic Abuse on Children (Chapter 5, Pages 35 - 46)

4.1 The Quiz

Tactic

1. Sulks
2. Tells me I am ugly
3. Causes a row when I want to go out
4. Denies he was abusive when challenged
5. Refuses to 'baby-sit'
6. Burns the breakfast
7. Threatens to report me to Social Services if I leave him
8. Rapes me when I am asleep

Answers

1. The Bully
2. The Headworker
3. The Jailer
4. The Liar
5. The Badfather
6. The King of the Castle
7. The Persuader
8. The Sexual Controller

IMPORTANT TO NOTE THAT THIS SESSION REQUIRES LOTS OF LOVING KINDNESS!

This session can be very painful. We may have experienced this as a child or we may be racked with guilt as adults. Facilitators must remind everyone that we did not do this to the children. He did!

When we ask, 'Why did I not leave before?' There is only one answer. That is, 'You left when you could. If you could have left earlier you would have done so'.

Be very aware that this may be the first time we realise how badly the children are affected.

4.2 Question Sheet for Session 4

What do children need?
Answer in the role to a pregnant mother.
The first group to consider is the pregnant mother, an unborn child and a newborn baby. What do they need? You may like to consider the needs of the mother first and then see that the other needs flow from them.

The next category deals with the needs of a six-year-old.
You can answer this as a mixture of the mother and the child.
Please list everything that you can think of that a six-year-old needs to develop successfully. Be specific. Don't just say things like 'care.' Define exactly what this means.

What does a teenager need?
Answer as both the teenager and the mother.
Consider whether the needs of the previous categories are linked to the needs of the teenager.

Effects of domestic abuse on children

Answer as the mother.

How is the first group affected by being exposed to domestic abuse?

Consider how the mother is affected and then discuss how this impacts on the unborn child and the new baby.

Now consider the six-year-old.

Answer as mother and child.

Consider that our child is now six years older. Remember all the effects on the first group. Now consider the situation six years later. See how much worse things are. Consider the beliefs our six-year-old will be developing.

Finally, now have a look at the teenager.

Answer as the mother and the teenager.

All the effects on the baby and the six-year-old have now accumulated in the teenager. How are they affected and what will they now believe?

Home improvements

Answer as the mother.

Now list how the lives of an unborn child, pregnant women newborn child are improved without the Dominator.

Imagine he has left or stopped being abusive when I am six months pregnant. I will then have the last three months without abuse. How will everything have improved for my new baby and me? Don't forget that I am attending the Freedom Programme and am receiving support and making friends.

Now list the improvements for a six-year-old.

Answer as the mother and the child.

He has left or changed when our child is five. We have been free of abuse for a year.

Now list the improvements for a fifteen-year-old.
Answer as both the mother and the teenager.
The dominator has left or changed when our child is thirteen. We have been free of abuse for two years.

Take the feedback then finish the session by reminding the group that the contents of this session are covered in pages 35 - 46 of 'Living with the Dominator'.

 freedomprogramme@btinternet.com
www.freedomprogramme.co.uk

Session 5. The Headworker (Chapter 6, Pages 47 - 56)

5.1 The Quiz

Tactic

1. Grits his teeth
2. Has affairs with other women
3. Has affairs with my friends
4. Says me I made him abusive
5. Denies paternity
5. Comes and goes as he pleases
7. Weeps on the doorstep
8. Ejaculates prematurely and blames me

Answers

1. The Bully
2. The Headworker
3. The Jailer
4. The Liar
5. The Badfather
6. The King of the Castle
7. The Persuader
8. The Sexual Controller

5.2 Question sheet for Session 5

Tactics of the Headworker.
Answer in the role of the Headworker.
How does the Headworker make me feel ugly, useless, stupid and mad?

What does the Headworker believe?
Answer in the role of the Headworker.
What does he believe about our competence and intelligence?
What does he believe women are placed on this earth for?
What is our function?

Where do such beliefs come from and how are they reinforced?
Answer in the role of the Headworker.
Consider language. What words are used about us to indicate that we are stupid?
What words indicate that we are pieces of meat?
Think of the history of psychiatry.
Think of magazines. Think of music and insidious messages in advertising. Think of a very famous radio presenter who consistently makes sexist jokes. Think about the content of jokes about women.

Which of these beliefs do women share?
Answer in the role of every woman.
Do I believe we are equal to men?
What words do **we** use about other women?

Effects of those beliefs on behaviour

Answer in the role of a woman.

How am I affected by living with a Headworker?

How am I affected by all his tactics?

How are we all affected by living in a society, which holds the beliefs of the Headworker?

How are we affected by our own shared beliefs?

The Confidence Booster

Answer in the role of the Confidence Booster.

How does the Confidence Booster behave to me?

What does he believe about women?

Take the feedback and read out the Nelson Mandela story on page 55 of 'Living with the Dominator'.

After the feedback from the Confidence Booster you can remind the group members that frequently states this fact

'You are absolutely fine just the way you are!' (This IS a fact!)

Now invite the group to repeat after you. 'I am absolutely fine just the way I am!' and give themselves a clap. Suggest that everyone stands in front of a mirror several times a day and repeats this mantra.

Remind everyone that the contents are covered on pages 47 - 56.

Session 6. The Jailer (Chapter 7, Pages 57 - 63)

6.1 The Quiz

Tactic

1. Displays weapons
2. Makes me feel guilty
3. Tells me my friends don't like me
4. Says it only happened because he was drunk
5. Says I can leave but the children stay
6. Says he "helps me" with the housework
7. Threatens to kill the children if I leave
8. Bribes me to have sex by offering to buy me a new winter coat

Answers

1. The Bully
2, The Headworker
3. The Jailer
4. The Liar
5. The Badfather
6. The King of the Castle
7. The Persuader
8. The Sexual Controller

6.2 Question sheet for Session 6

Tactics used by the Jailer

Answer as the Jailer.
How does the Jailor stop me seeing friends?
How does he stop me working?
How does he keep me in the house?
How does he cut me off from my family?

The Jailer's beliefs

Answer as the Jailer.
Where does the Jailor believe women should be?
What would he believe about a man who did not keep his partner locked away?
What does he believe we will all do if we *do* go out?
What does he believe we all are?

Where do all these beliefs come from and how are they reinforced?

Answer as the Jailer.
Consider language and commonly used phrases.
Consider social traditions, sports and education.
Think about social policies and advertisements.
When did women get the vote?

Which beliefs do women share?

Answer as every woman.
When I first meet the Jailer do I recognise his tactics as abusive?
If I do have a partner who is not a jailor, how would I speak of him?
E.g. '*He lets me go out!*' The use of the word 'Let' implies that I believe he has the right to give me permission.

How do our beliefs and experience affect our behaviour?

Answer as a woman.
How am I affected by being kept in the house?
How am I affected by being prevented from working?

How am I affected by being cut off from our friends and family?
How are we all affected by our widely shared beliefs?

The Liberator

Answer as the Liberator.
How does the Liberator behave? Consider his reactions to my desire to work, get out of the house and meet my friends?
How does he behave to my friends and family?
What does he believe about me?
Does he trust me?

Take the feedback and remind everyone that the contents are covered on pages 57 - 63 of 'Living with the Dominator'.

I am going to college

I form a standing circle and invite everyone to imagine that they are all my husbands. When we married, I left college to bring up the children on the condition that, when the children are old enough and if we have enough money,
I can go back.

They are now old enough and we are rolling in money and I greet you all on your return from work armed with my prospectus.

All my husbands must now use the tactics of the Dominator to persuade me not to go. When they have succeeded, I ask them to repeat the exercise and try to persuade me not to go to college **WITHOUT** using the tactics of the Dominator. If they do, I name the tactic, e.g. Liar or Headworker. The group soon realises that they cannot persuade me not to go to college without using abusive behaviour and therefore the very act of trying to do so is, in fact, abuse.

Finally, we repeat the exercise, but this time they are the Liberators, Confidence Boosters, etc... and I am going to college!

 freedomprogramme@btinternet.com
www.freedomprogramme.co.uk

Session 7. The Sexual Controller (Chapter 8, Pages 65 - 76)
7.1 The Quiz

Tactic

1. Stalks me
2. Makes me think I am going mad by moving furniture and then denying it
3. Goes everywhere with me
4. Says he was abusive because he was jealous
5. Asks the children to check up on me
6. Tells me I must be a lesbian if I say no to sex
   (Bless him! He thinks it is an insult!)
7. Ignores the housework until I do it
8. Promises that he will see a relate counsellor if I have him back

Answers

1. The Bully
2. The Headworker
3. The Jailer
4. The Liar
5. The Badfather
6. The Sexual Controller
7. The King of the Castle
8. The Persuader

Question sheet for Session 7

Note that the there are 3 separate questions about his tactics. Allow at least 5 minutes for each one then revert to the usual format for the rest of the questions.

Tactics of the Sexual Controller.

Answer as the Sexual Controller.
How does he make me have sex when I do not want it?
How does he use sex as a weapon to degrade and defeat me?
How does he use my love and desire for him to control me?

The beliefs of the Sexual Controller.

Answer as the Sexual Controller.
What does he believe about men and women?
What does he believe we are actually for?
Does he believe we have any other function apart from providing sex?
What does he believe about out rights and his rights?
Does he like women?

Where do these beliefs come from and how are they reinforced?

Answer as the Sexual Controller
Law. Media. Magazines. Newspapers. The medical profession. Fine art. Religion. Music. History. Give examples.

Which of these beliefs do women share?

Answer as every woman.
Do I believe we have a right to say no to sex?
If the answer to that is no, what do I believe is my function?
Do I believe I am a failure if I don't have a man?
Effects of the Sexual Controller on women.

Answer as a woman.
How am I affected by living with a sexual controller?
How are we all affected by living in a society which holds these beliefs?

The Lover

Answer as the Lover.
How does he behave sexually?
Does he show me affection?
What does he believe about women?
Does he like us?
Would he go to a lap-dancing club?
If not, why not?
What does he believe about sex?

Please note that the facilitator does not give an opinion about the lap-dancing club. Tell the groups that you do not expect them to be able to reach a consensus on this so you do not include it in the feedback. After the end of the feedback you can remind them that when I run mens programmes the men always say that a non abusive man would have too much respect for women to go to that sort of place.

Take the feedback and remind everyone that the contents are covered on pages 65 - 76 of 'Living with the Dominator'.

 freedomprogramme@btinternet.com
www.freedomprogramme.co.uk

Session 8. The King of the Castle (Chapter 9, Pages 77 - 86)

8.1 The Quiz

Tactics

1. Kicks walls

2. Does not use my name
3. Goes out without taking his key
4. Says he suffers from Gulf War Syndrome
5. Contradicts my instructions to the children
6. Pretends he can't cook
7. Says, 'Unless you have me back, I will follow you to the ends of the earth!'
8. Tells me I am unnatural if I refuse sex

Answers

1. The Bully
2. The Headworker
3. The Jailer
4. The Liar
5. The Badfather
6. The King of the Castle
7. The Persuader
8. The Sexual Controller

8.2 Question sheet for Session 8

Tactics of the King of the Castle

Answer as the King of the Castle.

The King of the Castle is subtle. He may not stomp in to our life and start ordering me around. How does he manipulate me so I will do all household tasks with out being aware of it?

How does he get me to do all the washing? How does he get me to do the cooking? How does he get me to do the cleaning? How does he make sure I know where things are and that I put things away? What is the question he will ask?

How does he get me to be in charge of menus? What question will he ask?

How does he begin to control the money? How will he ensure he is in charge of the television?

When all the tactics listed above have succeeded, he moves on to the next stage. He now openly starts to treat me as an unpaid servant. What will he now do?

The beliefs of the King of the Castle.

Answer as the King of the Castle.

What does he believe about the status of the occupation of housework?

What sort of people should therefore do his housework?

Would a "real man" pay someone to do his housework?

What does he believe about men who do their share of housework?

Where do these beliefs come from and how are they reinforced?

Answer as the King of the Castle.

Consider his childhood. Look at advertisements. Consider soap opera, films and books. What are women seen to be doing? Consider social policies and commonly used phrases which describe women?

 freedomprogramme@btinternet.com
www.freedomprogramme.co.uk

Which beliefs do we share?
Answer as every woman.
If I want my partner to do a household task, how do we phrase the request?
How will I react when he does not tidy up after himself?

How are we affected by the tactics used by the King of the Castle?
Answer as a woman.
How am I affected by being treated as a skivvy without rights or respect?
How are we all affected by the beliefs of the society in which we live?

How does the Partner behave?
Answer as the Partner.
He is the non-abusive counterpart to the King of the Castle. What does he do around the house and what does he believe?

Take the feedback and read 'The Good Wives Guide' from page 82.
Remind everyone that the contents of this session are covered on pages 77 - 86 of 'Living with the Dominator'.

Session 9. The Liar (Chapter 10, Pages 87 - 97)

9.1 The Quiz

Tactic

1. Swings his foot
2. Hides my shoes
3. Tells me I must be suffering from PMT
4. Says I must have him back because he has cancer
5. Says any red-blooded man would kill his wife if he found her in bed with another man
6. Hits me when the children are in the house
7. Has his own chair that no one else is allowed to use
8. Asks the surgeon to stitch me up tight after childbirth

Answers

1. The Bully
2. The Jailer
3. The Headworker
4. The Persuader
5. The Liar
6. The Badfather
7. The King of the Castle
8. The Sexual Controller

9.2 Question sheet for Session 9

The Liar and 'Rules of the Game'

Open the book at page 88 and look at 'Rules of the Game'. Then visit the 'Training' section on my web site and watch the DVD clip of me explaining the 'Rules of the Game'. Explain the whole graphic to the group. Before you go to ask them to write the answers, ask couple of group members of each small group to explain the graphic to the rest of their group. Allow between 5 and 10 minutes for this. Explain that you have asked them to do this as it will help them to understand the questions better when they come to answer them.

What are the Rules?

Answer as the abusive man.

Make a list of eight Rules of the Game. Use phrases like: "Women should..." "She should always..." "She should never..." I should be able to..." Write these rules in the voice of the Dominator.

Abusive Tactics

Have a look at the Dominator on page 11 and note an example of which aspect of the Dominator keeps which rule in place. For example, "She should never answer back" would be kept in place by the Bully. You can note the answers at the side of your rules above. Initials such as KOC (King of the Castle) will suffice.

Breaking the Rules

Answer in the role of a woman.

How do I break the rules? Don't forget that I often do not know what the rules are. One of the rules is that I should always know what the rules are. When considering how I break the rules, look at the list you have written. I could break each rule in many different ways, either accidentally or deliberately. This time write these examples in my voice, for example. 'I left him.'

 freedomprogramme@btinternet.com
www.freedomprogramme.co.uk

Excuses for Violence

Write his excuses in his voice.

Use emotive language and remember that he has not yet hit me. Do not spare the bad language. It will be easier for him to hit me if he convinces himself that I am not human.

Trying to put the rules back in place by using the tactics of the Liar

Answer in his voice.

How does he now get the rules back in place using Minimisation, Denial and Blame?

Give examples of the "only" word to make the abuse seem less than it was.

What will he say to deny that anything happened?

What will he blame? Make a list including as many medical conditions as possible. Don't forget that he will rarely give the real reason, which is that I broke the rules. He will, however, blame me. What will he say?

Which part of the cycle of "Rules of the Game" does he have to change to change his behaviour?

Is he actually angry or is all this manufactured outrage?

How does the liar's behaviour affect his victims?

How am I affected by all these complicated tactics?

The Truthteller

Answer in his voice.

An honest and accountable man. How does the opposite of the Liar behave?

Feedback

Seat the group in a large circle.

Return to the large group and tell everyone that they will now read back the "Rules" in the voice of the Liar. To get into the part, we all need to sit like him. Now, ask someone from each group to read one rule at a time with feeling.
Go round the circle as fast as you can and feel the atmosphere build up.

We do not ask the groups to read out which aspect of the Dominator keeps each rule in place. That was a useful revision exercise, which also increases our understanding of the whole process of power and control. We now go back to using women's voices and read out one example of how we broke a rule. Again, go round the circle fast and feel the atmosphere build up.

Now we have listed how we break the rules, we need to go back to the voice of the Liar and "wind him up." When you have read all the 'wind ups' out, you can do the role play.

Role Play

Place all the chairs in two rows facing each other.

The facilitator plays a woman whose abusive partner has been ordered by the court to attend a perpetrator programme. She now feels able to stand up to him.
A group member can play the man. When she stands up to him he says he is going out to cool off. He then walks up and down between the rows of chairs listening to the others all shouting out the thoughts that he is using to 'wind himself up'.

Ask him how he now feels and if he would have come back to hit us. When he has given himself enough excuses he will hit us and now we will list the minimisation denial and blame tactics of the Liar. Follow that with the effects on us and finish with our honest and accountable man.

Remind everyone that the contents of this session are covered on pages 87 - 97 of 'Living with the Dominator'.

Session 10. The Persuader (Chapter 11, Pages 99 - 109)

The Quiz

Tactic

1. Drives too fast
2. Tells me I am useless
3. Moves me to a strange town
4. Attempts suicide
5. Says I made him abuse me
6. Says I am a bad mother
7. Refuses to have sex with me
8. Complains if I spend money on myself

Answers

1. The Bully
1. The Headworker
3. The Jailor
4. The Persuader
5. The Liar
6. The Badfather
7. The Sexual Controller
8. The King of the Castle

 freedomprogramme@btinternet.com
www.freedomprogramme.co.uk

10.2 Question sheet for Session 10

Tactics of the Persuader

Answer in his voice.
How does he make me feel sorry for him?
How does he indicate to me that he cannot cope without me?
Will he also use other people to influence me?
How will he use the children to persuade me to have him back?
What threats or promises may he make?
How will he make me jealous in order to persuade me to have him back?
How will he use the excuses of the Liar to increase his level of control?

Beliefs of the Persuader

Answer in his voice.
Who does he believe is responsible for his behaviour and his well-being?
Does he believe he has to pay any price for his violence and abuse?
Does he believe his behaviour is in any way unacceptable? Who does he believe is allowed to end the relationship and whom does he believe is not?

Where do these beliefs come from and how are they reinforced?

Answer in his voice.
Consider popular music, country and western and blues.
Consider the law. Consider all the people he may go to for help. How might their responses reinforce his beliefs? For example, he may visit a bolloxologist for help to manage his *'anger'*.

Which beliefs do I share?

Answer as every woman.
Do I believe I am responsible for his well-being?

 freedomprogramme@btinternet.com
www.freedomprogramme.co.uk

How am I affected by The Persuader?
Answer as a woman.
How am I affected by being made to feel sorry for him?
How am I affected by his threats?

The Negotiator
Answer in his voice.
How does he behave if I want to end the relationship? Whose welfare will he consider? What does he believe?

Take the feedback and remind everyone that the contents of this session are covered on pages 99 - 109 of 'Living with the Dominator'.

 freedomprogramme@btinternet.com
www.freedomprogramme.co.uk

Session 11. Warning Signs (Chapter 12, Pages 113 - 116)

11.1 The Quiz

Tactics

1. Cracks his knuckles.
2. Takes the buggy in the boot of the car
3. Uses the word "woman" as an insult
4. Promises to go to anger management (bolloxology)
5. Makes jokes about me to the children
6. Asks,:"Where is my clean shirt?"
7. Visits a lap dancing club
8. Says he was abusive because he is insecure

Answers

1. The Bully
2. The Jailer
3. The Headworker
4. The Persuader
5. The Badfather
6. The King of the Castle
7. The Sexual Controller
8. The Liar

11.2 Question sheet for Session 11

The Bully
Make a list of the warning signs for the Bully. What will I be able to see in the first two weeks of the relationship?

The Jailer
Make a list of the warning signs for the Jailer. What will I be able to see in the first two weeks of the relationship?

The Headworker
Make a list of the warning signs for the Headworker. What will I be able to see in the first two weeks of the relationship?

The Persuader
Make a list of the warning signs for the Persuader. What will I be able to see in the first two weeks of the relationship?

The Liar
Make a list of the warning signs for the Liar. What will I be able to see in the first two weeks of the relationship?

The Badfather
Make a list of the warning signs for the Badfather. What will I be able to see in the first two weeks of the relationship?

The King of the Castle
Make a list of the warning signs for the KOC. What will I be able to see in the first two weeks of the relationship?

The Sexual Controller
Make a list of the warning signs for the Sexual Controller. What will I be able to see in the first two weeks of the relationship?

Sometimes we feel stupid because we failed to see these warning signs in the past. Don't! You did not have your 'Freedom Eyes' before but you will see clearly in the future.

11.3 My New Boyfriend

We can feed back from this session by pretending we have just met 'my new boyfriend' who is clearly a Dominator.

Take the feedback and remind everyone that the contents of this session are covered on pages 113 - 116 of 'Living with the Dominator'.

15689577R00028

Printed in Great Britain
by Amazon